The Endless Pendulum

Democracy, Right Wing, Left Wing, and the Sacred Conflict of Power

Ramkumar S P

First Edition: 2025

Disclaimer

This book is a work of political philosophy, social inquiry, and speculative reflection. The ideas, interpretations, and critiques presented herein are intended to provoke thought, stimulate discourse, and explore the cyclical nature of governance, ideology, and power across history and cultures.

The author holds deep respect for democratic values and constitutional frameworks, including the Indian Constitution. This book does not target or defame any specific government, political party, leader, religion, or institution. Any resemblance to current or past events or individuals is purely coincidental or used illustratively for educational discussion.

This work upholds the principles of intellectual freedom, and its purpose is to encourage democratic resilience, civic awareness, and ideological balance, not to incite division or promote extremism.

Preface

This book was born from a question that refused to stay quiet: Why does history seem to swing endlessly between ideologies, never settling, never satisfied?

As political tensions deepen across the world and democracies strain under the weight of polarization, it became clear that the conflict between Right and Left is not an aberration—it is a feature of power itself. I set out to understand this phenomenon not just through history or politics, but through human nature: identity, fear, ambition, inequality, and hope.

The Endless Pendulum is not a partisan work. It does not argue for one side over the other. Instead, it argues for the necessity of both, for the sacred tension that keeps democracy alive. Through this journey, I've come to believe that a healthy society is not one that silences its opposition—but one that protects it.

This book is for thinkers, sceptics, patriots, and students of power—anyone willing to ask: What if the survival of democracy depends not on winning, but on resisting the urge to destroy the other side?

I hope this book sparks dialogue, not division. I hope it encourages you not only to question, but also to build.

Welcome to The Endless Pendulum.

Content

Manifesto: The Eternal Cycle of Power

Democracy is not the natural state of mankind.
It is a rare and fragile flower, born from centuries of blood, betrayal, and dreams.

When democracy rises, it opens the gates to freedom —
"Freedom breeds ambition,
Ambition breeds wealth,
Wealth breeds inequality,
Inequality calls for order".
And under the banners of "tradition," "stability," and "patriotism," the right-wing reaction takes hold.

Right-wing forces, armed by capital and driven by fear, twist democracy into a tool for the few.
They do not destroy democracy with swords — they hollow it out from within.
Slowly, methodically, they weaken the spirit of the citizen and empower the oligarch.

But the hunger for justice does not die.
Out of the ruins, left-wing movements rise — angry,

righteous, vowing to tear down the old order.
Yet power, once grasped, knows no ideology.
Left-wing governments, in time, become the new capitalists.
They seize wealth in the name of the people, but use it to feed their own dynasties.
They silence dissent in the name of equality, but build new chains in secret.

Thus, democracy is betrayed again — not by one side, but by both.

And so the pendulum swings:
Democracy → Right-Wing Reaction → Left-Wing Rise → Democracy Reset → Repeat.

This is no accident.
It is the natural cycle of human society, as old as civilization itself:

"Hard times create strong men,
Strong men create good times,
Good times create weak men,
Weak men create hard times".

And so too:

"Democracy creates freedom,
Freedom creates inequality,
Inequality creates authoritarianism,
Authoritarianism creates revolution,
Revolution resets democracy"

The lesson is brutal but clear:
Without vigilance, democracy will always be devoured by the human hunger for identity, power, and wealth.
The only hope is to understand the cycle — to resist its darkest turns — and to forge a new age where democracy is not merely reset, but reborn stronger than before.

Chapter 1: The First Law — Survival

Before there was kingdom, tribe, or city, there was the trembling animal called Man.
He crawled under open skies, he was hunted by beasts, starved by winters, broken by storms.
In that ancient wilderness, there was no justice, no fairness, no mercy.

Only one law reigned supreme:

"Survive, or die".

Everything Man has ever built —

"Every tool, every fire, every shelter, every prayer, sprang from the primal terror of annihilation".

Survival shaped his instincts:

- **Fear** sharpened his senses.
- **Hunger** sharpened his mind.
- **Greed** sharpened his hands.
- **Lust** sharpened his bloodline.
- **Violence** sharpened his will.

Even today, in the glittering towers of modern cities,
beneath silk suits and endless screens,
the beast has not been tamed — only disguised.

"Every law is a survival strategy,
Every economy is a rationing strategy,
Every government is a shelter against chaos".

Survival — not goodness — was the original purpose of society.
"Not fairness,
Not happiness,
Not freedom,

First, survive,
Later, dream".

Before ideologies, before manifestos, before democracy and dictatorships —
humans gathered not out of love, but out of need.
To share fire. To defend land. To pass down genes.
And slowly, they wrote the first unspoken code of civilization:

"Together, we stand a better chance."

That was the beginning of politics.
Not noble, but necessary.
Not idealistic, but instinctive.

The Shadow Still Lurks

We like to believe we have evolved.
That we are moral creatures guided by ethics and law.
But scratch the surface of any nation in crisis,
and you will find this ancient law still pulsing underneath:

When threatened, people do not reach for compassion. They reach for control.

Survival justifies corruption.
Survival justifies violence.
Survival justifies tyranny — even in the name of peace.

And this is where the pendulum begins to swing.

Not with ideology.
Not with elections.
But with the elemental fear of losing everything.

Chapter 2: The Birth of Identity

Once Man secured his survival,
once the fire stayed lit through the night,
once the children were fed, and the predators held at bay—
he lifted his head above the mud and asked a question no animal had ever dared to ask:

"Who am I?"

It was the first moment of true consciousness.
No longer was existence defined merely by breath and hunger.
Now, it was defined by meaning.

The First Mirrors

At first, the answers were rooted in usefulness.

- He who brought the most food was admired.
- He who killed the greatest beast was revered.
- He who defended the weak was honoured.

Power, earned through strength, cunning, or wisdom, became the earliest form of identity.

Others looked at the strong man and thought:
"He is more than alive — he is important."
"He is not merely surviving — he matters."

Thus, admiration was born.
And from admiration came ambition.
And from ambition, competition.

Suddenly, to merely survive was not enough.
Now, Man craved significance.

The Great Splintering

The race for identity began.

Some shaped themselves through brute strength.
Some sought it in wealth — a surplus that spoke of success.
Others turned to knowledge, hoarding wisdom like warriors hoarded weapons.
Some bent to faith, claiming identity through the divine.
Still others clung to lineage, building legacies of blood and memory.

These paths, once personal, became tribes.
And tribes became classes, castes, clans, and eventually nations.

Each man's answer to *"Who am I?"*
became a collective anthem of *"Who are we?"* —
and, more dangerously,
"Who are they?"

The Double-Edged Gift

Identity gave humans culture, language, purpose, and vision.
It allowed civilizations to form, myths to flourish, and heroes to rise.
But identity also became the seed of division.

It built walls where there were once open plains.
It drew lines in the sand where there was once kinship.
It turned neighbours into strangers, and strangers into threats.

"Survival birthed Man.
Identity divided him".

The Battle for Meaning

From this point forward, all of human history would become a battleground of identity.

- *Who gets to define what matters?*
- *Who decides who belongs?*
- *Whose story becomes the truth?*

Whether through religion, race, ideology, or nationhood, the quest for identity would fuel empires and genocides, revolutions and renaissances.

And always — just beneath the surface —
the same ancient whisper remained:

"I want to be more than safe. I want to be seen."

Chapter 3: The Creation of Hierarchies

"Where there is identity, there is comparison.
Where there is comparison, there is pride.
Where there is pride, there is hierarchy".

Man, once content to merely live,
now began to measure the worth of his life by how it stood next to another.

"No longer was it enough to survive.
No longer was it enough to be someone".

Now, he asked:

- Who is stronger?
- Who is richer?
- Who is wiser?
- Who is purer?
- Who is more "chosen" by the gods?

Comparison became a scale.
Scales became rankings.
Rankings birthed power.

The First Thrones

"The strongest became the chief,
the oldest became the shaman,
the fertile became the bloodline,
the clever became the merchant,
and the violent became the king".

Society — once a circle of equals huddled around a fire — rose into a pyramid,
each step carved from the ambition of one
and the submission of another.

The top was narrow.
The base was wide.
Order was born.
But so too was oppression.

"Hierarchy promised stability.
But it demanded obedience".

Natural at First, Brutal Always

These early hierarchies felt natural, even necessary.

- The strongest protected the tribe.
- The wisest guided the tribe.
- The fertile sustained the tribe.
- The skilled enriched the tribe.

But nature does not guarantee kindness.
Strength became tyranny.
Wisdom became superstition.
Wealth became greed.

And slowly, the lines between earned respect and inherited dominance began to blur.

When Hierarchies Hardened

What began as practical structure ossified into sacred systems.

- Monarchies, justified by divine right — *"God chose my blood."*
- Aristocracies, protected by bloodlines and marriage — *"Purity must be preserved."*
- Caste systems, sanctified by religion — *"Your place was decided before birth."*
- Capitalist empires, guarded by armies and laws — *"If you can't pay, you don't belong."*

What was once flexible became rigid.
What was once functional became untouchable.

Inequality was no longer a side effect.
It was the blueprint.

The Lie of the Ladder

Every step up the ladder told the same lie:
"You earned this."
Every step down whispered a crueller one:
"You deserve this."

Those at the top called it merit.
Those at the bottom called it fate.
And somewhere in between,
the majority fought one another for the right to climb —
even if it meant stepping on each other's backs.

The Deep Truth

This is not corruption.
This is not failure.
This is not a mistake in the system.

This is the system.

Hierarchy is the instinctive response to identity.
It is not a flaw in civilization.
It is the foundation.

And yet,
"beneath every rebellion, every revolution, every dream of equality
—
there lies a yearning to be seen as equal,
even in a world that was built to say some are more".

Chapter 4: The Rebellion Against Hierarchy

For a time, hierarchies stood like mountains. Unquestioned. Unmovable. Sacred.

- Kings ruled because they were born to.
- Priests ruled because they spoke for the gods.
- Lords ruled because they held the sword.

The pyramid of power loomed above all, casting shadows over the lives of the many.

But power, once admired, eventually breeds resentment. The same eyes that once looked up with awe began to look up with anger.

The poor man looked at the prince and whispered:

"Why not me?"

The soldier bled for the general and cried:

"Who made him greater than I?"

The farmer bent under tax and asked:

"Is his blood gold, and mine mud?"

The Spark of Rebellion

Injustice — real or imagined — burns hotter than hunger.
The body can endure starvation.
But the soul revolts when humiliation becomes routine.

The lowly did not rise for bread alone.
They rose for dignity.
They rose to be seen.

- The slave wanted more than freedom — he wanted a name.
- The peasant wanted more than land — he wanted respect.
- The worker wanted more than wages — he wanted a voice.

Thus was born rebellion.

The ancient survival instinct — once directed outward at wolves and storms —
turned inward, against the kings, the priests, the landlords, the emperors.

The Collapse of the Pyramid

When the pyramid of power grows too steep,
it collapses under the weight of its own arrogance.

- Peasants rose with pitchforks against the castle.

- Slaves tore their chains and their masters.
- Citizens stormed palaces and guillotined kings.

What began as whispers became riots.
What began as hope became revolution.

Revolution became the final weapon of the powerless —
not just to survive,
but to matter.

The Left-Wing Instinct

From these ashes emerged a new fire: the Left-Wing instinct.

Born not in palaces, but in prisons.
Not in universities, but in the streets.
Not in scriptures, but in slogans.

It said:

- *"No man should rule another by birth."*
- *"The land belongs to those who till it."*
- *"The factory belongs to those who work it."*
- *"The wealth of the few is the theft of the many."*

While the Right-Wing instinct clung to hierarchy, order, and tradition, the Left-Wing instinct demanded equality, rebellion, and redistribution.

It was not just political — it was emotional.
It was not just economic — it was moral.

"If I am not free, no man shall be."

A Pendulum, Not a Ladder

History did not move forward like a ladder —
It swung, back and forth, like a pendulum.

- Hierarchies rose.
- Rebellions smashed.
- New orders formed.
- And inequality crept back in — quietly, inevitably.

Each new rebellion promised equality.
Each new government slowly rebuilt the pyramid it had destroyed.

Because the drive to survive, to matter, and to rise —
lives not just in kings and tyrants,
but in every man.

Chapter 5: The Invention of Democracy

The ancient war between rulers and the ruled had raged for centuries.

- Empires were built on bones.
- Kingdoms bloomed and fell like seasons.
- Blood wrote laws, and fire erased them.

Power — once taken, never yielded willingly —
was always met with resistance, rebellion, revolution.
But every revolt left a ruin.
And every ruin left a question:

Must we forever live in cycles — of tyranny, then terror, then tyranny again?

Must the only way to change power be to burn it down?

The Birth of an Idea

Out of this exhaustion — not utopia — came a fragile miracle:
"Democracy".

It did not rise from the top.
It rose from the bottom, from the weary feet of peasants,
from the bloodied backs of rebels,
from the quiet thinkers who dreamed not of palaces,
but of a shared table.

Democracy asked:

- Can power be divided, before it divides us?
- Can we rule ourselves, without becoming each other's tyrants?

It was not born in a single place.
It emerged like fireflies in the dark —
in city-states like Athens, in councils of tribes, in scattered republics that flickered and died.

But the modern idea — of a nation governed by its people,
of laws above rulers, of votes above swords —
that was new.
That was revolutionary.

Democracy: A Weapon Against Power

Democracy was not a celebration of human instinct.
It was a rebellion against it.

Because instinct says:

- *"Might is right."*
- *"The strong should rule."*

- *"Obey or be crushed."*

But democracy said:

- *"Every voice matters."*
- *"Every person counts."*
- *"Power must answer to the people."*

It replaced the king's decree with the citizen's ballot.

It turned succession by bloodline into elections by choice.

It transformed revolutionary violence into peaceful transition.

The pyramid of society remained —
but it no longer rose into the clouds, unreachable.
It flattened, just enough, to let the many breathe.

A Ceasefire, Not a Victory

Democracy was not the end of the human struggle.
It was a pause in the war.

A ceasefire —
between the powerful and the powerless.
Between instinct and reason.
Between order and freedom.

It was not built on conquest,
but on rules — agreements between enemies.

- That we would fight with words, not weapons.
- That power would be borrowed, not seized.
- That truth would be pursued, even if never found.
- That the minority would lose today — but be safe to try again tomorrow.

It was not perfection.
It was a fragile truce.

The Fragile Foundations of Democracy

But democracy has enemies — not always outside, but within.
Because it demands what humans most struggle to give:

- Trust — in strangers.
- Restraint — in victory.
- Dignity — in defeat.

It depends on:

- Winners who do not become tyrants.
- Losers who do not become arsonists.
- Citizens who endure disagreement without violence.
- Institutions that outlast their founders.

Without these, democracy is not simply weak —
it is doomed.

Because beneath every democratic system,
the old instincts still sleep —
the instinct to dominate, to silence, to conquer.

And if democracy falters,
those instincts will return —
not as shadows, but as rulers.

Chapter 6: Inequality

Inequality: The Core Human Condition

Long before nations were carved into maps, before laws tamed violence into order, one brutal truth ruled humanity:

"Some had more. Some had less".

Inequality was not invented by kings or priests.
It was birthed in the marrow of existence itself.

- Some ran faster.
- Some fought harder.
- Some dreamed bigger.

Civilization merely polished the brutal fact:
Freedom magnifies inequality.

The more liberty a society grants, the more brutally it reveals the differences hidden within its people.

Thus, every new system — every revolution — every democracy — faces the same demon:
"The relentless return of inequality".

Right-Wing Rule: Institutionalizing Inequality

The Right-wing does not apologize for inequality.
It sanctifies it.

*"Hierarchy is nature's order.
The strong must lead.
The weak must obey."*

Under Right-wing ideologies:

- Wealth becomes virtue.
- Power becomes proof of worth.
- Tradition becomes a shield against change.

Freedom exists — but it is a selective freedom:
Freedom for the strong.
Freedom for the dominant.
Freedom for the favoured.

The poor are scolded.
The marginalized are ignored.

The nation becomes a fortress protecting privilege, disguised as protecting "freedom."

"In the name of liberty, Right-wing systems often enthrone aristocracy".

They do not solve inequality.
They *codify it.*

Left-Wing Rule: Fabricating New Inequality

The Left-wing rises not to preserve inequality, but to obliterate it.

"We must level the field.
We must tear down the thrones.
We must liberate the masses."

But in the fiery rush to equalize all things:

- The individual is crushed by the collective.
- Ambition is condemned as greed.
- Dissent is labelled treason.

Wealth is seized.
Industries are nationalized.
Freedoms are traded for guarantees.

Yet power, like water, seeks its own level.

Soon:

- The party elite replace the old nobility.
- Bureaucrats become the new masters.

Freedom dies under the weight of enforced "equality."
And a new, colder hierarchy emerges — more rigid because it dares not name itself.

"In the name of justice, Left-wing systems often enthrone tyranny".

They do not eliminate inequality.
They *disguise it* under slogans.

Democracy: A Fragile Hope Between Extremes

After the storms of Right and Left, democracy rises once more like a fragile dawn.

"Let the people rule themselves."
"Let freedom breathe."

True democracy offers a different vision:

- Rights for all.
- Voice for all.
- Opportunities open to every soul.

It does not promise equality of result — only equality of opportunity.

It trusts that citizens, left free, will find a fairer balance between ambition and compassion.

Yet democracy is fragile.
Freedom, left unchecked, grows wild:

- The strong pull ahead again.
- The clever hoard opportunity.
- The rich whisper in the ears of rulers.

Democracy, too, breeds inequality — but more slowly, more invisibly.

And so, the cycle threatens to begin again.

The Eternal Return of Inequality

Right-wing rule institutionalizes inequality.
Left-wing rule reinvents inequality.
Democracy tries to restrain it — but often fails.

"Inequality is not a flaw in the system.
It is the system".

It is born from human instincts:

- To strive.
- To dominate.
- To protect what one has earned — or stolen.

History changes the costumes.
Human nature writes the script.

The banners of freedom and equality wave bravely — but beneath them, the same ancient dance continues:

"The dance of hunger, ambition, fear, and pride".

Chapter 7: Identity Crisis and the Collapse of Trust

The Fracture of the Soul

When inequality blooms unchecked, it does not only gnaw at people's wallets.
It gnaws at their *sense of self.*

In the mirror of society, individuals ask:

"Who am I?"
"Where do I belong?"
"Why am I left behind?"

When answers are unclear or painful, identity — that fragile construction — *fractures.*

Out of that fracture rise:

- Tribalism
- Extremism
- Rage

The invisible threads that once bound citizen to citizen *snap.*

"Without shared identity, there can be no shared destiny".

And once identity fractures, *trust dies*.

The Collapse of Trust

Trust is the oxygen of democracy.
Without it, the system suffocates.

In the collapse:

- The poor distrust the rich.
- The rural distrust the urban.
- The educated mock the traditional.
- The traditional resent the progressive.

Each group builds its own truth.
Each group brands the others as enemies.

Institutions once trusted — government, media, science — become battlegrounds of suspicion.

"They are lying to you."
"They are stealing from you."
"They are plotting against you."

Conspiracies bloom like weeds.
Facts become opinions.
Opinions become weapons.

The Search for New Identity

Amid the chaos, humans do what they have always done: *"They search for belonging"*.

Some join:

- Nationalist movements.
- Revolutionary cults.
- Religious extremism.
- Rigid ideological tribes.

The new identities promise:

"You are not alone."
"You are special."
"You are chosen."
"You are the victim — and the avenger."

These new identities offer clarity — but at the cost of compassion.

They offer strength — but at the cost of freedom.

"The group becomes the self.
The enemy becomes the obsession".

The Threshold of Violence

When trust collapses and identity radicalizes, the final threshold appears:

"Violence".

Violence between classes.
Violence between tribes.
Violence between citizens and the state.

It may begin with words — venomous, unrestrained.
It may escalate to protests, insurrections, purges.

When the mirror of society shatters completely, the blood follows.

History's darkest chapters all begin the same way:

- *Inequality ignored.*
- *Identity fractured.*
- *Trust betrayed.*
- *Violence unleashed.*

The Abyss Stares Back

Nietzsche warned:

"Whoever fights monsters should see to it that he does not become a monster. And if you gaze long into an abyss, the abyss also gazes into you."

In the collapse of identity and trust, societies do not merely fall.
They *transform* — often into the very tyrannies they once feared.

Without identity rooted in *common humanity,*
Without trust rooted in *shared truth,*
Freedom rots.
Equality perishes.
Democracy dies.

Chapter 8: The Rise of Extremes and the Savior Myth

In the Ashes of Trust

When the structures of trust collapse, when the old identities dissolve into dust, a terrible hunger rises in the human heart. A hunger for *certainty*, for *meaning*, for *something unshakable* in a world crumbling under its own contradictions.

And from that hunger, two monsters are born.

One wears the mask of *purity*.
The other wears the mask of *salvation*.

Both whisper the same lie:

"Follow me. I will save you."

And the people, desperate for hope, listen.

The Extremists: Purity or Death

Extremists thrive on broken dreams.

The fascists call for blood to cleanse the nation.
The revolutionaries promise paradise through destruction.
The zealots vow holy wars to purge the unbelievers.

Moderates are ridiculed as cowards.
Compromisers are branded as traitors.
Dialogue becomes impossible. Only screams remain.

"If you are not with us, you are against us."

Cities burn. Families shatter. Nations tear themselves apart from within.
The extremists do not seek to heal —
They seek to rebuild the world by first burning it to ashes.

The Saviors: Chains in Disguise

As chaos spreads, the second monster rises:
The Saviors.

They come with promises, not with guns.
Smiling faces. Soothing voices.
Corporations offering security. Governments offering order.
Charismatic leaders offering themselves as the *only solution.*

"Give me your freedom — and I will give you safety."

The people, tired of uncertainty, give up their rights.
They surrender debate for obedience.
They trade liberty for protection.

And the saviours build cages so beautiful,
the people forget they are trapped inside.

The Mirror: Extremes and Saviors Are Twins

On the surface, the extremists and the saviours seem to be enemies.
In truth, they are twins —
born of the same fear, fed by the same desperation.

- Both demand absolute loyalty.
- Both crush dissent.
- Both despise the messy chaos of true freedom.

And both lead society not to salvation, but to ruin.

The left wing, the right wing, the capitalist, the revolutionary —
they all fall into the same trap:
Promise salvation, deliver control.

In their hands, democracy becomes a hollow word,
freedom becomes a memory,
and the human spirit bends under invisible chains.

"The greatest trick tyranny ever played was convincing the people it was their only hope."

The Betrayal of Hope

There is no sadness greater than the betrayal of hope.

It is one thing to be defeated by an enemy.
It is another, darker thing to be betrayed by the very dreams that once inspired you.

The extremists and the saviours both betray the people —
but they do it with promises, not with swords.
They sell slavery as destiny.
They brand obedience as patriotism.

And the people, desperate and blind,
pay for their illusions with their souls.

Chapter 9: Fear, Identity, and the Rise of Manufactured Enemies

The Nature of Fear

- Human beings are hardwired for survival.
- Fear was once a useful instinct — warning of predators, dangers, enemies.
- But in organized societies, fear can be manipulated.
- Leaders and demagogues learn to *engineer fear* to hold power.

Fear is no longer a warning. It is a tool.

Identity Under Threat

- Identity gives humans belonging and pride.
- When people feel their identity is threatened (culturally, economically, politically), they seek protection.
- Leaders create "us" and "them" to offer that protection.

- Minorities, reformers, foreigners become symbols of that "threat."

Manufacturing the Enemy

- Historical Examples:
    - Jews in Nazi Germany.
    - Migrants and Muslims in far-right Europe.
    - Communists and academics during McCarthyism.
    - Bourgeois and intellectuals during leftist purges (e.g., Cultural Revolution).
- The Method:
    - Dehumanize.
    - Stereotype.
    - Isolate.
    - Attack.

An enemy created is a people controlled.

Right-Wing Weaponization of Fear

- Right-wing governments often rise during instability.

- They present themselves as defenders of tradition, culture, nationhood.
- They frame minorities or dissenters as existential threats.
- Fear is used to justify authoritarianism, censorship, violence.

Left-Wing Mirrors: Fear of the "Class Enemy"

- Leftist regimes, once in power, often replicate the same behaviour.
- They fear "capitalist subversion," "reactionary forces," "counter-revolutionaries."
- Purges, censorship, and ideological purity become the tools of survival.
- In trying to protect the revolution, they betray it.

Fear corrupts both left and right.
No ideology escapes it.

How Fear Kills Democracy

- Fear makes people abandon reason.
- Fear makes people accept loss of rights for "safety."
- Fear polarizes society into camps of hatred.

- Fear justifies tyranny, both from the majority and the state.

A frightened society votes itself into chains.

The Real Enemy is Within

- The collapse of democracy, the rise of authoritarianism, the cycles of left and right — they are not driven by the minorities.
  They are not driven by the "other."

They are driven by our own fears —
by our failure to master them.

Freedom dies not by attack from without,
but by surrender from within.

Chapter 10: The Road to Tyranny — Why People Choose Their Chains

The Crisis of Confidence

Democracy, in its finest form, promises dignity, debate, and destiny shaped by the people themselves.
But democracy is fragile.
It demands patience, tolerance, and faith — all of which erode under pressure.

When crises strike — economic collapse, cultural confusion, mass migrations, pandemics —
the people's faith in the slow machinery of democracy crumbles.
Arguments replace solutions.
Gridlock replaces progress.

A frightened people do not seek more freedom.
They seek protection.

And when the system no longer protects them,
they look for someone who will.

The Fearful Heart

Human instincts are older than civilization.
In the primal mind, uncertainty is danger; difference is threat.

In the beginning, fear warned of predators.
In modern times, fear warns of *others* — immigrants, minorities, dissenters, thinkers, reformers.

When societies are healthy, fear is managed by reason.
When societies are weakened, fear mutates into rage, hatred, and desperate tribalism.

Fear demands an enemy.
Fear demands a leader.

And it finds both.

The False Savior

Into the chaos steps the strongman.
He speaks not of compromise, but of conquest.
Not of listening, but of punishing.

He offers a simple message:

- *"You are good."*
- *"They are bad."*
- *"Follow me, and I will destroy your fears."*

He dresses himself in the symbols of the nation.
He wraps his lies in the language of truth.
He promises salvation — but only if freedom is sacrificed.

The people cheer.
The people vote.
The people chain themselves willingly.

The Manufactured Unity

In democracy, differences are celebrated.
In tyranny, differences are crushed.

The strongman cannot allow opposition, for opposition reminds the people that they still have choices.

Thus, the work begins:

- Control the media.
- Purge the universities.
- Imprison the dissenters.
- Redefine patriotism as obedience.

Minorities are labelled as traitors.
Critics are accused of being enemies.
The nation becomes a mirror reflecting only the leader's face.

Unity is achieved — by silencing all other voices.

The Last Vote

Ironically, the death of democracy often comes not through tanks in the street,
but through ballots in the box.

People vote away their own rights.
They applaud the destruction of their courts, their press, their parliaments.

They believe they are saving their nation.
They do not realize they are digging its grave.

By the time they understand,
it is too late.

The constitution is a corpse.
The laws are shackles.
The revolution devours its own children.

The Aftermath

When the strongman no longer needs the people,
he turns against them too.

- Jobs vanish.
- Freedoms vanish.
- Dignity vanishes.

What remains is silence, fear, and the endless memory of a freedom they once held but could not protect.

And the saddest truth of all:

"The people were not conquered.
They surrendered".

Chapter 11: The Need for Left-Wing Movements

When Chains Become Intolerable

Authoritarianism thrives on fear, but it cannot eliminate suffering.

Under the weight of oppression, even the most obedient citizens begin to feel the cracks:

- Hunger that promises are not feeding.
- Injustice that loyalty is not protecting.
- Dreams that even obedience cannot fulfil.

Soon, silence becomes unbearable.
Submission becomes humiliation.

Every dictatorship writes its own death sentence — it simply cannot predict when it will be read.

And in the ashes of despair, a question emerges:
"Is this all there is?"

The Awakening of Conscience

The first rebellion is not on the streets.
It happens in the heart.

- Workers whisper in factories.
- Students question in classrooms.
- Artists hide their truth in songs and paintings.
- Mothers tell their children stories of what once was — and what could be.

It is not political yet.
It is human.

It is the simple realization:

"We deserve better."

This awakening is not organized, not ideological — yet.
But it lays the seeds for the left-wing spirit: the defence of dignity, equality, and freedom against tyranny.

The Return of Collective Hope

Right-wing regimes exalt the individual when it suits them — but crush collective action.

Left-wing movements, in their truest form, arise to rebuild what authoritarianism destroys:

- Solidarity.
- Compassion.
- Shared destiny.

No longer is the citizen alone, afraid, silent.
Together, they find the courage to dream.

They organize unions.
They form cooperatives.
They write manifestos.

Not because they are promised power —
but because they are reclaiming their humanity.

Hope, once shared, becomes unstoppable.

The Left as Corrective Force

In history, left-wing movements often emerge not as conquerors, but as correctors.

They are the counterweight to unchecked greed, unearned privilege, and institutional cruelty.

Their demands are ancient:

- Food for the hungry.
- Education for the poor.
- Medicine for the sick.

- Justice for the oppressed.

Where right-wing tyranny stratifies and divides, the left seeks to heal and unify.

It does not always succeed.
It can fall into its own extremisms.
But at its purest, *the left exists because injustice exists.*

Without it, suffering would have no voice, and power would have no rival.

The Cycle Reignited

The rise of left-wing movements reignites democracy's heartbeat:

- Strikes become speeches.
- Speeches become votes.
- Votes become laws.

And slowly, the balance of fear tilts toward the people once more.

Yet even here, the seeds of future struggle are sown — because power, once seized, must always be watched.
Even liberators can be tempted.

Thus, the cycle continues:
Freedom won, freedom endangered, freedom defended again.

Eternal vigilance is the price of liberty.

Chapter 12: The Betrayal Within — How the Left Turns Against Its Own People

From Liberation to Domination

Every revolution begins by promising justice, equality, and dignity.
But the moment power is seized, a dangerous transformation can occur.

The leaders who once fought for "the people"
now claim to be the people.

Criticism becomes betrayal.
Dissent becomes treason.
Diversity of thought — once celebrated — becomes a threat to the fragile new order.

Thus, the liberators forge new chains.

The Fatal Flaws of Revolutionary Power

Why does this betrayal happen?
Several ancient forces awaken once power is in left-wing hands:

- *Purity Spiral:*
  True believers demand that everyone conform perfectly to the ideology.
  Any deviation, any question, is seen as counter-revolutionary.
- *Centralized Control:*
  In trying to create equality, left-wing regimes often centralize economic, political, and even cultural power.
  But centralized power breeds corruption, inefficiency, and paranoia.
- *Fear of Counter-Revolution:*
  Having risen from struggle, left-wing leaders often see enemies everywhere.
  They respond not with debate — but with purges, prisons, and executions.
- *Myth of the "New Man":*
  Left-wing revolutions often believe they can "re-educate" humanity into perfect beings.
  Those who refuse to change are seen not as fellow citizens, but as obstacles to be removed.

Historical Echoes

- *The French Revolution:*
  Robespierre, champion of liberty, turned France into a blood-soaked tyranny during the Reign of Terror.
- *The Soviet Union:*
  Lenin's revolution against tyranny became Stalin's nightmare of purges, gulags, and mass starvation.
- *Mao's China:*
  The Cultural Revolution, meant to "purify" society, unleashed mobs, destroyed culture, and murdered millions.
- *Cuba, Venezuela, Cambodia:*
  In every case, a movement that promised empowerment delivered poverty, fear, and dictatorship.

The oppressed become oppressors when they forget that power must be questioned, even their own.

The Psychology of Betrayal

- *Moral Certainty:*
  "We are good, they are evil."
  This black-and-white thinking blinds leaders to their own cruelty.

- *Fear of Losing Gains:*
  Leaders justify repression by claiming it protects the revolution.
  "Temporary measures" become permanent terrors.
- *The Cult of the Leader:*
  The revolution becomes a religion.
  The leader becomes a god.
  The people become obedient disciples — or enemies.

The Collapse from Within

A left-wing government that betrays its own ideals rots from the inside:

- Innovation dies.
- Trust evaporates.
- Citizens flee — in body, spirit, or both.

Eventually, the regime either:

- Becomes indistinguishable from the tyranny it overthrew,
- Or collapses under the weight of its lies.

In the ruins, a broken people are left to rebuild again — if they can.

Lessons Forgotten, Lessons Remembered

The left-wing betrayal is not inevitable.
But it is inevitable when power is unchecked.

"Democracy", "transparency", "humility" — these are the antidotes.

The left must remember:

- It is not the saviour of the people.
- It must always be the servant of the people.

Without this wisdom, every revolution risks becoming another chapter of betrayal.

Freedom is not won once.
Freedom must be won every day.

Chapter 13: How Democracy Blooms Again

Ashes of Betrayal, Seeds of Renewal

History teaches a cruel truth:
Freedom is often buried before it is reborn.

- After the terror of authoritarianism,
- After the collapse of broken promises,
- After the betrayals of right-wing or left-wing extremes,

ordinary people — not heroes, not saviours — quietly begin the work of rebuilding.

The dream of democracy never truly dies.
It smoulders beneath the rubble, waiting for air.

Humble Beginnings

Democracy does not return with fireworks or grand speeches.
It starts small:

- Secret meetings in basements.

- Underground newspapers.
- Songs sung in secret.
- Parents teaching their children stories of freedom.

And when the tyrants weaken, when the fear lifts —
the people emerge, blinking into the sunlight.

Their first act is not to rule.
It is to speak.
It is to remember.
It is to demand a voice.

The Pillars of New Democracy

A true democratic rebirth requires rebuilding key pillars:

- *Rule of Law:*
  Laws must apply to all — rulers and ruled alike.
- *Independent Institutions:*
  Courts, press, universities — free from government control — ensure power is questioned.
- *Freedom of Speech:*
  Without fear of punishment, truth can flourish again.
- *Civic Participation:*
  Voting, protesting, debating — democracy thrives when citizens do not stay silent.

- *Checks and Balances:*
  Power must be divided, challenged, and limited.

"Freedom without structure is chaos.
Structure without freedom is tyranny.
Democracy needs both".

Healing the Wounds

A broken nation cannot simply "move on."

Democracy blooms only when society confronts its own pain:

- Acknowledging crimes of the past.
- Offering justice for victims.
- Creating systems that protect minorities, not persecute them.
- Teaching history honestly, without myth or shame.

Without healing, old hatreds fester.
Without justice, old wounds reopen.

Fragile Yet Beautiful

New democracies are fragile:

- Economic crises can tempt people back into authoritarianism.
- Charismatic leaders can seduce them with easy lies.
- Fear can again silence truth.

But fragile does not mean weak.

Like a young tree after a fire, democracy grows stronger with every storm it survives.
It sends deeper roots into society:

- In art.
- In literature.
- In law.
- In the hearts of children.

Each generation must protect it — or lose it.

"Democracy is not a gift from the wise.
It is the achievement of the brave".

The Eternal Struggle

Democracy is never "finished."
It is never "safe."

Every election, every law, every protest, every debate — these are the battles through which democracy survives.

It requires:

- Patience in defeat.
- Courage in dissent.
- Humility in victory.

The cycle may tempt us toward tyranny again.
But knowledge, vigilance, and solidarity can slow the cycle — even break it.

The dream is not perfection.
The dream is the endless, beautiful effort to become better.

Wherever people gather to speak freely,
to argue openly,
to vote without fear —
there, democracy blooms anew.

Chapter 14: The Sacred Conflict — Why Democracy Needs Both Right and Left

The Illusion of Purity

Throughout history, nations have been seduced by purity:

- A purely right-wing government promising limitless growth.
- A purely left-wing government promising perfect equality.

Both dreams become nightmares.

Without balance, right-wing rule decays into oligarchy and exploitation.
Without balance, left-wing rule decays into stagnation and tyranny.

Democracy's true genius is that it refuses purity.
It *demands conflict.*
It *forces balance.*
It *welcomes tension.*

The Driving Force: Vision and Growth (Right-Wing Capitalism)

The right-wing instinct, at its best, provides:

- *Vision*: Ambitious goals — cities to build, industries to create, frontiers to conquer.
- *Dynamism*: Risk-taking, entrepreneurship, bold investments.
- *Efficiency*: Cutting through bureaucracy to deliver results.
- *Pride*: Reviving national identity, inspiring people to achieve greatness.

Without this force:

- Societies stagnate.
- Dreams shrink.
- Innovation dies.
- Nations fall behind.

Right-wing energy feeds the engine of development.

The Protective Force: Justice and Conscience (Left-Wing Restraint)

The left-wing instinct, at its best, provides:

- *Protection:* Shielding workers, minorities, and the vulnerable from exploitation.
- *Conscience:* Questioning whether the vision serves all, not just the few.
- *Regulation:* Creating labour laws, environmental protections, and social safety nets.
- *Inclusion:* Expanding democracy beyond the elite, giving voice to the marginalized.

Without this force:

- Power becomes unchecked.
- Inequality widens into cruelty.
- Communities are sacrificed for profit.
- Nature itself is destroyed.

Left-wing vigilance defends the soul of society.

A Government Without Tension is a Government of Tyranny

When one ideology dominates, democracy withers:

Pure Right-Wing Rule	Pure Left-Wing Rule
Wealth is hoarded	Innovation is strangled
Minorities are crushed	Dissent is punished
Nature is destroyed	Economic collapse looms
Society splits into masters and slaves	Society collapses into grey uniformity

Tension between the two sides is not a flaw — it is democracy's engine.

The *right* pushes forward.
The *left* pulls back.
The *centre* holds — if we are wise enough to protect it.

Case Study: Labour Laws and Worker Protections

Right-wing vision built the industries.
Left-wing pressure built the labour protections.

- Without leftists, factories would have continued child labour and deadly conditions.
- Without capitalists, there would be no factories — no jobs — no wealth to share.

Thus:

- Labour laws emerged not as charity but as compromise.

- Minimum wages, safe working conditions, unions — all won by struggle, but under the canopy of capitalism.

Left and right dance together, often angrily — but if either leaves, the music stops.

What a Balanced Democracy Looks Like

A healthy democracy features:

- *A right-wing vision* ambitious enough to dream big.
- *A left-wing conscience* courageous enough to call out injustice.
- *A neutral law* that ensures neither side can dominate permanently.
- Elections where both sides can win — and lose.
- Courts where ideology bows before justice.
- Media where all views battle in open sunlight.

The goal is not permanent peace.
The goal is managed conflict.
The goal is creative tension.

The Eternal Warning

When either right or left decides:

- *"We are the only truth,"*
- *"We will destroy the other,"*

the balance shatters.
Democracy dies.
The cycle of tyranny returns.

Thus:
We must *protect tension itself.*
We must *protect the argument.*
We must *protect the other side, even when we hate them — because their existence keeps us free.*

In the garden of democracy, conflict is the sunlight.
Difference is the rain.
Together they grow freedom.

Chapter 15: The Fall of the Sacred Conflict

Democracy, at its heart, is not a celebration of unity.
It is a celebration of sacred conflict — a constant, living tension between opposing visions, between ambition and compassion, between freedom and equality.

But the sacred conflict is fragile. It survives only when both sides — Right and Left — accept each other's legitimacy. The day one side decides the other is not simply wrong, but evil, democracy's slow death begins.

The Fragile Balance

At the height of a healthy democracy, citizens may argue, protest, and passionately disagree, but they share an unspoken vow:
We are all still one people.
The right to disagree, the right to dream differently — that is the soul of democracy.

But when fear takes root, that vow weakens.
When ambition burns too hot, that vow shatters.
And then, the sacred conflict, once beautiful, turns into a battlefield of destruction.

How the Right-Wing Destroys the Balance

History teaches us that when right-wing forces grow unchecked, democracy suffers in predictable ways:

- *Demonization of Opposition:* Political rivals are not simply criticized — they are declared traitors, foreign agents, or enemies of the state.
- *Seizure of Institutions:* Courts, police, media — once neutral guardians — are seized and bent to favour one ideology.
- *Economic Capture:* Wealth concentrates into the hands of a few, who use it not to build but to dominate. Wealth becomes not a symbol of success, but a weapon against dissent.
- *Militarization and Fear:* Minorities, immigrants, and outsiders are portrayed as existential threats, justifying repression and violence.

Historical echoes:

- Europe's collapse into fascism in the 1930s.
- The brutal dictatorships of Latin America in the 1970s.

In every case, the Right's quest for purity and power murdered the sacred conflict — and with it, freedom itself.

How the Left-Wing Destroys the Balance

But unchecked left-wing power is no gentler.
When the Left forgets its own soul, it too tramples democracy underfoot:

- *Moral Absolutism:* The Left begins to see itself as the only righteous force, branding opponents not as rivals, but as oppressors undeserving of even a voice.
- *Suppressing Free Markets:* Innovation and enterprise are crushed under the heavy weight of bureaucracy and suspicion.
- *Silencing Dissent:* Artistic, academic, and political freedom are sacrificed at the altar of ideological purity.
- *Collapse of Incentive:* When reward is severed from effort, society withers. Creativity and ambition decay.

Historical echoes:

- Stalin's Soviet Union.
- Mao's China during the Cultural Revolution.

In every case, the Left's crusade for enforced equality poisoned the sacred conflict — and turned liberation into tyranny.

The Psychology of Collapse

The collapse of democracy does not begin with tanks in the streets.
It begins inside the human heart:

- *Fear* makes citizens crave strongmen.
- *Hate* blinds them to their neighbour's humanity.
- *Despair* convinces them that only extremism can save them.

Fear + Hate + Despair = The Death Spiral of Freedom.

By the time the final freedom is lost, it feels almost inevitable — as if it was never truly there.

The Inevitable Tyranny

When the Right-wing dominates unchecked, democracy withers into fascist dictatorship.

When the Left-wing dominates unchecked, democracy drowns in totalitarianism.

Both paths lead to the same graveyard:

- Freedom murdered.
- Truth silenced.
- Humanity shackled.

The Pattern of History: Slow, Then Sudden

Every dying democracy follows the same grim pattern:

- *First:* Laws are quietly bent, twisted to favour one side.
- *Then:* Opposition is demonized, labelled as dangerous or subhuman.
- *Then:* Minorities are persecuted under the guise of protecting the nation.
- *Then:* Elections become meaningless theatre.
- *Finally:* The people awaken one day to find they are no longer free — and wonder how it happened.

"How did we fall?" they will ask.
The answer will be: *"We chose fear over freedom. We chose hate over hope."*

Examples are carved into the bones of history:

- Weimar Germany,
- Venezuela,
- Modern-day Hungary and Turkey.

Final Message: Guard the Sacred Conflict

The sacred conflict is not a curse.
It is the guardian of freedom.

True patriots defend the right of their rivals to exist.
True citizens accept the tension because they know it protects against tyranny.
True visionaries build bridges, not fortresses.

Democracy does not die from invasion.
It dies from betrayal within.

The sacred conflict must never be abandoned.
It must be nourished, defended, and, when wounded, healed — not erased.

Chapter 16: The Rise of the False Patriot

In every age, when the sacred balance of democracy trembles, a new figure emerges from the shadows — not the tyrant we easily recognize, but the *False Patriot.*
He wears the flag on his chest, speaks of honour and loyalty, yet his heart beats not for freedom, but for dominance.

"The false patriot does not love his country; he loves himself wearing the mask of the country".

Where democracy demands patience, debate, and tolerance, the false patriot demands obedience, purity, and silence.
He turns disagreement into treason, dissent into betrayal.
He builds walls where bridges are needed, and names his own ambition as "national salvation."

The Psychology of the False Patriot

The false patriot emerges from deep fears:

- *Fear of Change:* As societies grow diverse and complex, the false patriot clings to a mythic past.
- *Fear of the Other:* Differences — in race, religion, opinion — are painted as existential threats.

- *Fear of Loss:* Economic shifts, social reforms, cultural evolutions are seen not as progress, but as theft.

The false patriot speaks to these fears, amplifies them, and then presents himself as the only cure.

Weapons of the False Patriot

The false patriot conquers not first through violence, but through manipulation.
His tools are ancient:

- *Language:* He redefines patriotism as loyalty to him alone.
- *Symbols:* He drapes himself in flags, sacred texts, and national heroes, claiming sole ownership.
- *Scapegoats:* He blames minorities, intellectuals, immigrants, and the media for the nation's woes.
- *Emotion:* He replaces reasoned debate with rage, pride, and resentment.

In his mouth, noble words rot.
Freedom becomes submission.
Strength becomes cruelty.
Unity becomes uniformity.

The False Patriot's Fatal Error

What the false patriot never understands is this:
A nation without honest dissent is not strong — it is hollow.
A democracy where fear rules is already half dead.
By silencing his fellow citizens, the false patriot does not save the nation; he poisons its heart.

Ultimately, his triumph is always temporary.
The seeds of resistance begin to grow in the silence he enforces.
Truth, crushed for a time, rises anew.

The Greatest Threat to a Democracy

The greatest threat to a democracy does not come from outside — it is born within, when those entrusted to protect freedom instead seek to *own* it.
The False Patriot is not just a villain in history books.
He lives wherever fear is stronger than hope, wherever power is valued above principle.

"Only a True Patriot — the Guardian of Freedom — can stand against him".

And it is to this rare and sacred soul we now turn.

Chapter 17: The True Patriot — Guardian of the Other's Right to Exist

In an age where the False Patriot thunders with empty pride, another figure stands quietly, almost invisibly:
The True Patriot.
A rarer, braver soul — not one who seeks to dominate his country, but one who chooses, every day, to serve its spirit.

The True Patriot does not measure love of country by the number of flags waved, nor by the decibels of his anger.
He measures it by how well he defends the *freedom of those he disagrees with.*
For he knows: *a nation's greatness lies not in uniformity, but in its wild, stubborn, chaotic diversity.*

The Sacred Duty: Protecting the Opponent

The True Patriot recognizes a truth others fear:

- If you silence your enemy today, you may lose your own voice tomorrow.
- If you crush the minority today, you invite your own oppression tomorrow.

Thus, the True Patriot stands not only for his rights but for the rights of those he opposes.
He fights for the existence of the Other — the critic, the dissenter, the outcast — knowing that without them, his own freedom is worthless.

The true measure of patriotism is how fiercely you defend the rights of those you wish would disappear.

Qualities of the True Patriot

The True Patriot knows that real loyalty to one's country sometimes demands opposing one's own party, challenging one's own leader, even risking one's own popularity.
Following are the virtues of a true patriot.

Virtue	How It Manifests
Courage	Speaking out when it is dangerous, standing up for unpopular truths.
Restraint	Refusing the temptation to silence or destroy political rivals.
Vision	Seeing the nation as an eternal conversation, not a fixed creed.

Love	Loving the messy, imperfect, ever-evolving country — not a fantasy version of it.
Sacrifice	Being willing to lose short-term victories for long-term freedom.

The True Patriot in History

Across ages and continents, true patriots often suffered in their lifetimes:

- *Socrates,* defending the right to question.
- *Abraham Lincoln,* urging unity and mercy even amid civil war.
- *Nelson Mandela,* forgiving those who imprisoned him, to build a future together.

They were mocked as traitors, fools, or dreamers.
But history remembers them differently: as *foundations,* not destroyers.

The Ultimate Truth: Patriotism Without the Other Is Not Patriotism

When the True Patriot looks at a political opponent, a minority, a critic, he does not see an enemy to be crushed. He sees a citizen whose existence makes the nation alive.

He understands:
Freedom for me, but not for you, is not freedom at all.
Justice for my side, but not yours, is not justice at all.
Victory without respect for the Other is the beginning of tyranny.

Thus, the True Patriot does something harder than fighting:
He coexists.
He endures disagreement.
He protects those who would not protect him.

And in doing so, he protects the invisible threads that bind a democracy together.

A nation survives not by the size of its army, nor the noise of its crowds, but by the unseen daily acts of True Patriots. Those who, quietly, stubbornly, choose to be the guardians of freedom — even when no one applauds them.

In the end, the sacred duty of every citizen is not just to love their country, but to love its unfinished, untidy, unruly promise:
The promise that *all of us* — even those we dislike — belong.

Chapter 18: The Eternal Vigil — Why Democracy Needs Constant Defence

Democracy is not a natural state.
It is a deliberate, fragile construction — a structure that stands only because people *choose* to defend it, generation after generation.

Unlike tyranny, which grows like a weed when left unchecked, democracy is a delicate garden.
It requires constant weeding:

- Weeding out greed,
- Weeding out corruption,
- Weeding out apathy,
- Weeding out the slow creep of unchecked power.

Why defence is Eternal

- *People forget.* Freedom, once won, feels inevitable.
- *People get tired.* Eternal vigilance is exhausting.

- *People get tempted.* Power offers easy rewards to those willing to trade liberty for security.
- *People seek simple answers.* Democracy demands patience, complexity, and uncomfortable debate.

Thus, *the erosion always begins in comfort* — not in crisis.

"Those who expect to reap the blessings of freedom must, like men, undergo the fatigue of supporting it."
— Thomas Paine

What Must Be Defended?

1. *Freedom of Speech* — even for the unpopular, the offensive, the minority.
2. *Separation of Powers* — courts, legislature, executive kept distinct and independent.
3. *Free and Fair Elections* — not just voting, but real competition and transparency.
4. *Rule of Law* — no one, not even the leaders, stands above the law.
5. *Peaceful Transfer of Power* — without bloodshed, without vengeance.
6. *Education of Citizens* — to think critically, to resist demagoguery.

The Role of the True Patriot

A *True Patriot* does not worship power.
A *True Patriot* does not blindly obey.
A *True Patriot* questions, protests, demands accountability — even when his own side is in power.

Because he knows:

- It is not the *leader* he defends.
- It is not the *party* he defends.
- It is *the principle* he defends —
  The principle that no man is born master, and no man born slave.

Final Warning

Democracy dies not when it is attacked from without.
It dies when citizens within *stop caring, stop speaking, stop fighting* for it.

Thus, the ancient warning:

"The price of liberty is eternal vigilance."

There is no final victory for democracy — only the eternal struggle to keep it alive.

Chapter 19: The Dream of the Balanced Republic

Throughout history, humanity has dreamed not merely of power, nor merely of freedom,
but of balance.

The Balanced Republic is that dream made flesh:
A system where ambition fights ambition,
where visionaries are restrained by guardians,
where the wings of progress are steadied by the weight of conscience.

The Ancient Origins of the Dream

In the rocky hills of ancient Athens, the first sparks were lit:

- Citizens gathering in assemblies, daring to govern themselves.
- Leaders elevated not by blood, but by persuasion.
- Laws written not for kings, but for all.

But even Athens fell — torn between demagogues and oligarchs, between war fever and internal decay.

Later, the Roman Republic rose — more cautious, more structured:

- Two consuls instead of one king.
- A Senate to counter the populists.
- Tribunes to protect the commoners from the aristocrats.

Rome too would fall, when ambition outweighed duty, and liberty drowned in the blood of civil wars.

The Lessons Engraved in Blood

History carved a brutal lesson into the memory of humanity:

- *Freedom without order breeds chaos.*
- *Order without freedom breeds tyranny.*
- *Only balance can endure.*

Thus the greatest architects of republics — from Cicero to Jefferson — understood:
The goal is not the elimination of conflict, but the management of sacred conflict.

The Roles in the Republic

- *The Right-Wing Visionary —*
  Dreams of greatness, expansion, achievement.
  Builds cathedrals, founds empires, fuels invention.
  But left unchecked, he will exploit, dominate, and destroy.
- *The Left-Wing Guardian —*
  Defends the vulnerable, demands justice, calls for accountability.
  Fights for workers, the environment, the forgotten.
  But left unchecked, he will suffocate innovation, punish excellence, and descend into tyranny of sameness.
- *The True Patriot —*
  Ensures both exist.
  Fights for the *conversation,* not for one side's permanent rule.
  Knows that destroying the other side is suicide for the republic itself.

The Fragile Dream

The Balanced Republic is the most unnatural of human achievements.
It demands that people restrain their worst instincts even when they have the power not to.

It demands:

- That winners show mercy,
- That losers accept defeat without bloodshed,
- That power be divided, contested, and shared.

It is, in many ways, a miracle.

And like all miracles, it must be guarded — not once, but every day.

The Republic Endures

When the right-wing visionary reaches too far,
the left-wing guardian must pull him back.

When the left-wing guardian grows too zealous,
the right-wing visionary must challenge him anew.

Back and forth.
Tension, struggle, compromise, renewal.

This sacred conflict is the heartbeat of freedom.

Thus, the Balanced Republic does not seek peace through domination —
It seeks peace through *managed conflict.*

It knows:

- That man will always hunger for power,

- That ambition will never die,
- That identity will always divide us.

And so it builds a system where *ambition checks ambition,* where *no identity rules forever,* and where *the dream of liberty survives another day.*

"A true patriot is not the servant of a faction, but the defender of the republic itself — ensuring even his rivals live to fight another day."

Thus, we guard the republic.
Thus the dream endures.

Chapter 20: The High Cost of Freedom

Democracy is a flower that blooms only in blood-soaked soil.

Throughout most of human history, men lived not as citizens, but as subjects.
They bowed before kings, emperors, warlords, or priests.
Their lives, their labour, their children — all belonged to the throne.

To be born free was a miracle.
To create freedom where none existed — an act of *revolutionary defiance.*

The Iron Grip of Monarchy

For centuries, monarchy seemed inevitable:

- *Power concentrated* in the hands of the few.
- *Obedience enforced* by sword and superstition.
- *Tradition glorified* to keep the masses from dreaming of change.

The king was God's anointed.
The emperor was fate's chosen son.
To resist was blasphemy — and often suicide.

Even when monarchies collapsed, they were often replaced not by democracy, but by *new tyrants.*

Napoleon followed the French Revolution.
The Bolsheviks replaced the Russian Tsar with a new dictatorship.
The cycle of thrones continued.

The Battle for Democracy

To carve democracy out of tyranny required:

- Bloodshed beyond imagination,
- Sacrifices from generations who would never see the fruits of their labor,
- Courage from ordinary men and women facing extraordinary cruelty.

The American Revolution.
The French Revolution.
The long, brutal struggles in South America, India, Africa.

Each victory was fragile.
Each democracy born was incomplete, imperfect, easily corrupted.

But still, it was a beginning.

Why We Must Protect It

Democracy is slow.
It is messy.
It disappoints.
It frustrates.

It allows fools to speak and criminals to run for office.
It tolerates injustice longer than it should.

But democracy has one sacred advantage:

It allows peaceful correction without the need for blood.

It gives the people — through struggle, protest, and persistence — the tools to remake their government without burning the world to ash.

Once lost, democracy is brutally hard to regain.
History shows this:

- Once a strongman seizes the throne,
- Once fear replaces debate,
- Once citizens become subjects again,
  It may take centuries for freedom to return — if it ever does.

Thus the great truth:

"It is easier to keep a democracy alive than to resurrect it from the grave."

The Duty of Every Generation

Each generation must decide:

- Shall we defend this flawed, fragile miracle called democracy?
- Or shall we throw it away in anger, apathy, or blind loyalty to a would-be king?

The battle never ends.
The temptation of easy answers, strong rulers, and suppressed freedoms never dies.

Thus, true patriots know:

- Even if the system is flawed,
- Even if change is slow,
- Even if leaders disappoint —
  Democracy is worth defending.

Better to extend its life a day longer, a year longer, a generation longer —
than to kneel again before a tyrant.

The Eternal Choice

In every age, in every nation, the choice stands:

- Freedom, with all its flaws, its burdens, its responsibilities?

- Or submission, in exchange for the false comfort of chains?

The republic may be wounded.
The democracy may be limping.
But it still stands.

And so long as it stands, so too does hope.

Chapter 21: The Eternal Conflict Within Us

Before the wars raged between Right and Left, before flags were waved and constitutions were signed, the true battlefield was born inside the human soul.

Long before governments, there was the first human —
Yearning to be free, yet desperate for safety.
Dreaming of endless possibility, yet craving the comfort of belonging.

This contradiction is ancient.
It is the first division.
It is the original war.

The Two Hungers

Inside every human heart, two forces struggle:

- *The Hunger for Freedom*
  The wild, roaring instinct to live as one chooses.
  To break old chains.
  To rebel.
  To create.
- *The Hunger for Belonging and Order*
  The deep, aching need to be part of something stable.

To feel protected.
To be anchored in tradition, history, and community.

Neither hunger is wrong.
Both are essential.

But when one dominates unchecked, it leads to destruction:

- *Freedom without Order* becomes chaos.
- *Order without Freedom* becomes tyranny.

Thus, humanity staggers forever forward — never fully satisfied, never truly whole.

The Birth of Ideologies

When the first tribes formed, when the first kings rose, when the first philosophers argued under ancient skies —
they were answering the question:
Which hunger matters more?

Over centuries, this eternal question birthed ideologies:

- *The Right-Wing:*
  Defenders of Order, Tradition, Hierarchy, Stability.
- *The Left-Wing:*
  Champions of Freedom, Equality, Progress, Revolution.

Each ideology is an imperfect answer to the perfect tension inside us.

Each speaks to one side of our soul —
and tempts us to forget the other.

Democracy: The Fragile Compromise

Democracy is not a victory for Freedom alone.
Nor is it a triumph of Order alone.

It is a fragile, stubborn, beautiful compromise between the two.

It says:

"We will let you dream.
But we will ask you to obey certain laws."

"We will protect your right to rebel with words.
But we will not let you tear down the house with violence."

"We will celebrate your uniqueness.
But we will bind you into a shared destiny."

Democracy understands the human soul better than any system before it.
It does not try to erase the conflict.
It *sacralises* it.

The Danger of Forgetting

When a society forgets the hunger for Freedom, it slides into tyranny.
When it forgets the hunger for Order, it collapses into anarchy.

When citizens believe only their side has value —
They betray themselves.

They deny the full spectrum of their own humanity.

Thus, the eternal conflict within must not be "won" —
It must be *endlessly managed, respected, and honoured.*

The battle between Right and Left is not a flaw.
It is not a sign of weakness.

It is proof that humanity is still alive, still striving, still human.

Inside each of us, the sacred war continues.
And in that struggle — in that beautiful tension — civilization moves forward.

Let us never curse the conflict within us.
Let us *thank it.*

Chapter 22: The Duty of the Citizen

If democracy is the delicate bridge between freedom and order,
then the *citizen* is the architect, the builder, the guardian, and the repairman of that bridge.

Without citizens who understand their role,
without citizens who accept their sacred duty,
the bridge collapses.

The Dream of Citizenship

To be a citizen in a democracy is not a mere accident of birth. It is not just a piece of paper called a passport.

It is a *living vow.*

A citizen promises:

- *To protect freedom* — not only their own, but their neighbour's.
- *To obey laws* — even when inconvenient, for the sake of the whole.
- *To stay informed* — to think, to question, to learn.

- *To speak out against tyranny* — whether it wears a left-wing cloak or a right-wing crown.
- *To compromise* — to accept that perfection belongs only to gods, not to governments.

A citizen is not a consumer of democracy.
A citizen is a co-creator of democracy.

The Four Pillars of Citizenship

1. *Vigilance*
   Freedom must be guarded.
   Tyranny grows fastest when no one is watching.
2. *Participation*
   Elections are only a small part.
   Debate, protest, volunteering, holding leaders accountable — these are sacred acts.
3. *Humility*
   Know that your side is not always right.
   Know that those who disagree with you are still your brothers and sisters in this grand experiment.
4. *Courage*
   The courage to speak when it is unpopular.
   The courage to listen when it is uncomfortable.
   The courage to defend the democracy even when your personal interests would gain from its fall.

The Grave Mistake

When citizens forget their duty,
they become consumers of government –
only caring what benefits they can harvest.

They grow lazy, entitled, outraged by inconvenience but silent at injustice.

In such times, *democracy rots from the inside.*
No army, no king, no tyrant is needed – the people themselves surrender.

The True Patriot

A true patriot does not blindly worship their nation.
A true patriot questions, critiques, reforms – precisely because they love it.

A true patriot ensures that both right-wing and left-wing voices survive.
Even when his own faction holds power, he protects the existence of the opposition.

Because the true patriot knows:

Without conflict, there is no democracy.
Without struggle, there is no freedom.
Without opposition, there is no life in the body politic.

The greatest danger to a democracy is not its enemies abroad.
It is the apathy, arrogance, and ignorance of its own citizens.

Democracy is not a guarantee.
It is a living thing, tended by the hands of millions.

Each citizen is a guardian of a fragile miracle.
Each citizen is a thread in the tapestry that stretches across generations.

When you stand as a citizen,
you stand in the footprints of those who fought and died for the right to choose their leaders.

When you fail as a citizen,
you betray not only yourself —
but all who will come after.

The duty of the citizen is sacred.
It is hard.
It is beautiful.

And it is the only thing standing between freedom and the long dark night of tyranny.

Chapter 23: When Democracy Becomes a Faith

In the end, democracy is not just a system.
It is not merely voting booths, legislative houses, or constitutions inked in law.

Democracy is a belief.

A belief that *every human voice has worth.*
A belief that *power must be shared, not seized.*
A belief that *truth can emerge through conflict, not be silenced by it.*

The Religion of Reason

Faith is not always about gods.
Sometimes it is about principles so sacred they demand devotion.

- Democracy believes in *the invisible authority of the people.*
- It trusts that *debate is holy,* and that *dissent is not sin but sacrifice.*
- It believes *no single man or party owns truth.*

It is, in essence, the *religion of reason,*
where *rituals are elections,*
priests are lawmakers,
and *heresy is tyranny.*

But like any faith — democracy can be corrupted.

The Fragility of Belief

When democracy becomes blind worship,
it risks becoming dogma.

When the system is seen as unbreakable,
people stop defending it.

When freedom is mistaken for license,
people exploit it to suppress others.

When opposition is seen as evil,
people seek to purge, not persuade.

A democracy that loses its soul becomes an empty cathedral.
A nation of citizens becomes a mob of zealots.

Faith Without Works Is Dead

Even the most beautiful belief,
if not acted upon,
dies in silence.

Democracy demands *faith in each other.*
And it demands *action.*

- Holding leaders accountable is an act of prayer.
- Compromise is an act of faith.
- Listening to your opponent — is a ritual of humility.

Without these, democracy rots.

The Pilgrimage of Nations

All nations walk this pilgrimage —
from tyranny to rebellion,
from chaos to constitution,
from freedom to forgetfulness.

Some return.
Some are lost.

But those who survive —
are those who never forget
that democracy is not given,
but *reborn every generation*
through belief, through struggle,
and through *sacred disagreement.*

Democracy is a faith — in the people, in truth, in the process.
Not perfect. Never complete. Always fragile.

But when citizens hold it close,
defend it fiercely,
question it bravely,
and pass it forward —

It becomes eternal.

Chapter 24: The Last Day of the Republic

No republic falls in a single day.
The fall begins in silence.
In laughter at broken rules.
In yawns at stolen power.
In shrugs when truth is twisted.

And then one day —
it is gone.

The temples of law still stand.
The flag still flutters.
The anthem still plays.

But the soul has fled.
And tyranny has moved in —
not with an invasion,
but with an invitation.

How the Republic Dies

1. *The Rise of the Strongman*
   He says what others won't.
   He promises greatness.
   He shatters norms — and the people cheer.

2. ***The Weakening of Institutions***
   Courts bend.
   The press is silenced.
   Law is weaponized.

3. ***The Demonization of Dissent***
   The opposition is no longer wrong — they are traitors.
   Critics are enemies.
   Dissent becomes disloyalty.

4. ***The Collapse of Trust***
   Truth is fragmented.
   Every fact has an agenda.
   The people no longer believe — in the system, in each other, in reality itself.

5. ***The Final Choice — or Its Absence***
   Elections become theatre.
   Or worse, they disappear.
   The people whisper: "At least the trains run on time."

Echoes from History

- *Rome* handed itself to emperors after the Senate became a farce.
- *Weimar Germany* mocked itself into the arms of fascism.

- *Chile, Egypt, Hungary, Venezuela* — all wore democratic masks before the blade fell.

Democracies do not die at gunpoint.
They die with applause.

What the Last Day Looks Like

It may not be fire and tanks.
It may be quiet — a law passed in the night.
A journalist disappeared.
A protest outlawed.
A phrase like: *"Only I can fix it."*

The republic does not scream.
It sighs.

And then — it is no longer ours.

The Warning

"The price of liberty is eternal vigilance." – Thomas Jefferson

The fall of the republic is never inevitable.
But neither is its survival.

Each citizen must be a sentinel.
Each generation must pass the torch — still lit, not smouldering.

There will come a day when the republic is threatened.
Not by invasion,

but by *forgetfulness,*
by *comfort,*
by *fear,*
by *hate.*

And on that day,
those who remember
must stand.

Because if not —
there will be no one left to remember at all.

Chapter 25: The Torch and the Tomb

At the end of every age, a decision awaits.
What shall we carry forward?
And what must we bury so it never rises again?

This is the moment between ruin and renewal.
A moment every generation must face.
Will we build monuments to the past,
or become architects of the future?

This is the chapter of reckoning —
between the torch and the tomb.

The Torch: What We Must Carry

1. The Idea of Human Dignity
Every law, every government, every ideology must begin here:
No person is beneath justice.
No voice is beneath hearing.

2. The Habit of Listening
Not for the sake of agreement,
but to understand before we oppose.
Dialogue is not weakness — it is civilization.

3. The Balance of Power

Right-wing dreams push us forward.

Left-wing caution keeps us human.

Together, they pull the cart of democracy forward.

4. The Will to Question Our Own Side

True patriots criticize their own tribe.

Blind loyalty builds nothing but graves.

5. The Fire of Memory

History, when forgotten, returns as nightmare.

We carry its lessons as torchlight in the dark.

The Tomb: What Must Be Buried

1. The Worship of Power

When leaders become gods, nations become graves.

2. The Poison of Identity Hatred

No homeland ever thrived by dividing its own people.

3. The Greed That Consumes the Commons

Land, water, labour — when hoarded, these kill civilizations.

4. The Echo Chamber of Certainty

A society where no one changes their mind is a society already dead.

5. The Fear of the Other

Fear has a purpose — but when it replaces thought, it destroys truth.

Between Inheritance and Innovation

The next generation inherits more than laws.
They inherit the consequences of what we carried —
and the curses of what we refused to bury.

Will we pass them a torch that burns bright,
or a tombstone etched with warnings we ignored?

The Eternal Responsibility

Freedom is not a gift — it is a torch.
Each hand that holds it must decide:
Do I carry it higher?
Or let it flicker out?

Justice is not automatic — it is built, breath by breath.
Every society that thrives learns to rebuild it every single day.

Democracy is not a resting place — it is a road.
And on that road, we walk — or we vanish.

**

Between the torch and the tomb stands every citizen.
Every vote, every act of courage, every refusal to hate —
is a hand reaching toward the light.

Carry it.
Pass it.
Protect it.

Or stand among the ruins.

Chapter 26: The Last Question

What is it all for?

Why endure the weight of freedom, the agony of choice, the burden of coexistence, the fragility of democracy?
Why not give in to the strongman?
Why not choose comfort over chaos, submission over struggle, silence over truth?

This is the last question.
And every generation must answer it — not with words, but with life.

The Hunger for Order

Tyranny is simple.
It promises:
I will think for you.
I will fight for you.
I will protect you — from others, from yourself, from the truth.

And for many, that is tempting.
Because freedom is terrifying.
Responsibility is exhausting.
Democracy is chaos — it is work.

But when you trade liberty for simplicity,
you lose not only your chains —
you lose your soul.

What Democracy Demands

It demands patience when you're angry.
It demands hope when you're tired.
It demands you defend the rights of those you disagree with
—
because if theirs can be taken, so can yours.

It demands you see your enemy as human.
It demands you stand up, not for your side — but for *the rules of the game.*

It demands imperfection, and offers *possibility.*

The Real Revolution

The true revolution is not in burning palaces or storming capitals.
It is in choosing dialogue over violence.
Nuance over dogma.
Balance over dominance.

The real revolution is living freely — *without needing a tyrant or a saviour.*

The Last Question Is This:

Can we live together — without trying to conquer each other?

Can we accept that no ideology will save us?
That truth has many voices,
and justice requires constant work?

Can we reject the lie that the other side must be destroyed?

If the answer is yes — even whispered, even imperfect — then there is hope.

Can we be The Circle Breakers?

Chapter 27: The Circle Breakers

Epilogue – Holding the Line

History repeats. But only when we fall asleep.

We've seen the arc.
Democracy breathes life into a nation.
Fear and power twist it into control.
Revolution burns away the old — only to become the new oppressor.
And from the ashes, democracy stumbles forward again.

The circle spins.
But it doesn't have to.

The Circle Breakers

They are not the loudest.
They don't chant in mobs or rule through fear.
They stand quietly at the edge of extremes,
guarding the middle ground that no one fights for — but everyone needs.

They are teachers, judges, journalists, citizens.
They ask inconvenient questions.

They defend unpopular truths.
They vote not for power, but for balance.

And they understand one sacred truth:

A true patriot ensures the survival of the opposing idea.

Because the moment one side eliminates the other,
democracy dies —
and tyranny, in whatever form, takes its place.

We Need Both Fires

- The *right-wing visionary* who dares to build, to grow, to dream.
- The *left-wing conscience* who holds them accountable, ensuring people are not trampled under profit.

One creates momentum.
The other draws boundaries.
Together — restrained by democracy — they push society forward without tearing it apart.

This conflict is not a flaw.
It is sacred.

Why You Matter

You are not a spectator in this cycle.
You are a gear in the machine, a hand on the lever, a vote on

the scale.
Whether you speak, write, teach, create, or simply *pay attention* — you shape the rhythm of history.

If enough of us refuse the extremes, hold fast to truth, and
guard the space between,
the circle won't spin — it will evolve.

Stand with the weak — or stand for what is right?
Do both.

Stand for what is right — even when it's hard to see.
And when in doubt, stand with the weak.
That's where the truth is often buried.
That's where justice begins.

A Final Vow

We, the Circle Breakers,
refuse to let democracy fall quietly.
We will not hand our future to tyrants wrapped in flags or slogans.
We will not cheer when our enemies are silenced.
We will not close our eyes when corruption wears our team's colours.
We will build. We will resist. We will question. We will hope.

And most of all —
we will keep the line alive.

For as long as it takes.
For as many times as needed.
Until the circle breaks — for good.

The Right looks to seize power from democracy.
It slides in quietly — when fear rises and opportunity appears.
But even the mighty Right can fall, and it falls only to a greater force —
the anger of the people, the rise of the Left.
And after the storm, when the dust begins to settle,
the people long not for vengeance — but for liberation.
That is when democracy begins to bloom again.
It takes time.
Sometimes decades.
Sometimes generations to regain the democracy.

Glossary of Key Terms

Anarchy: A state of lawlessness or political disorder due to the absence of governmental authority.

Authoritarianism: A system of governance characterized by strong central power and limited political freedoms.

Capitalism: An economic system based on private ownership of the means of production and their operation for profit.

Democracy: A political system in which power is vested in the people, who rule either directly or through freely elected representatives.

Hierarchy: A system in which people or groups are ranked one above the other according to status or authority.

Ideology: A system of ideas and ideals, especially one that forms the basis of economic or political theory and policy.

Inequality: The unequal distribution of wealth, opportunity, or status within a society.

Left Wing: A political position associated with progressive reform, social equality, workers' rights, and redistribution of wealth.

Liberty: The state of being free within society from oppressive restrictions imposed by authority.

Right Wing: A political position typically associated with tradition, hierarchy, capitalism, national identity, and limited government intervention.

Revolution: A forcible overthrow of a government or social order, in Favour of a new system.

Tyranny: Cruel and oppressive government or rule by a single leader or elite group.

Personal Note from the Author

Hope you enjoyed reading this work.
This book is a reflection of thoughts that have been bothering me for a long time — questions about power, identity, democracy, and the cycles we repeat.

I wrote this not to impose ideas, but to encourage conversation without hesitation, to promote questioning without judgment, and to invite answers without obligation.

Even if you don't agree with everything in these pages, I hope it offered you a new idea, a shift in perspective, or simply something worth thinking about.

As this is my debut work, I took the support of advanced writing tools. However, every argument, every intention, and every conviction within it is my own.

Thank you for giving your time, attention, and trust to a first-time author.
It means more than words can say.

— **Ramkumar S P**

www.ingramcontent.com/pod-product-compliance
Lightning Source LLC
Chambersburg PA
CBHW022157160726
48282CB00024B/231
* 9 7 8 9 3 3 4 3 3 6 5 3 5 *